ACKNOWLEDGEMENTS

Publishing Director   Piers Pickard
Publisher   Tim Cook
Commissioning Editor   Jen Feroze
Illustrator   Pippa Curnick
Designer   Hayley Warnham
Print production   Larissa Frost,
                             Nigel Longuet

Thanks to   Dr Kim Bryan, Jennifer Dixon

Published in February 2016 by Lonely Planet Global Limited
ABN 36 005 607 983
ISBN: 978 1 76034 038 4
www.lonelyplanetkids.com
© Lonely Planet 2016
Printed in Malaysia

10 9 8 7 6 5 4 3 2

Lonely Planet Offices

AUSTRALIA
The Malt Store, Level 3, 551 Swanston St,
Carlton, Victoria 3053 T: 03 8379 8000

IRELAND
Unit E, Digital Court, The Digital Hub,
Rainsford St, Dublin 8

USA
150 Linden St, Oakland, CA 94607
T: 510 250 6400

UK
240 Blackfriars Rd, London SE1 8NW
T: 020 3771 5100

STAY IN TOUCH lonelyplanet.com/contact

FSC
www.fsc.org

MIX
Paper from
responsible sources
FSC™ C021741

Paper in this book is certified against the
Forest Stewardship Council™ standards.
FSC™ promotes environmentally responsible,
socially beneficial and economically viable
management of the world's forests.

Lonely Planet Kids

LET'S EXPLORE
JUNGLE

Pippa Curnick

Are you ready for an adventure?
Two explorers, Marco and Amelia, are going deep into the rainforest, and they've invited you to come too!

The best explorers need to be ready for anything. Look at the list below and add stickers to the next page to get ready to go! Cross the items off the list when you've stuck them on.

JUNGLE KIT

MARCO
* Shirt
* Cargo pants
* Walking boots
* Backpack
* Camera

AMELIA
* Long-sleeved T-shirt
* Cargo pants
* Walking boots
* Bug spray

This map of the world shows where the planet's rainforests are located. Every one of these areas of forest contains some wonderful wildlife.

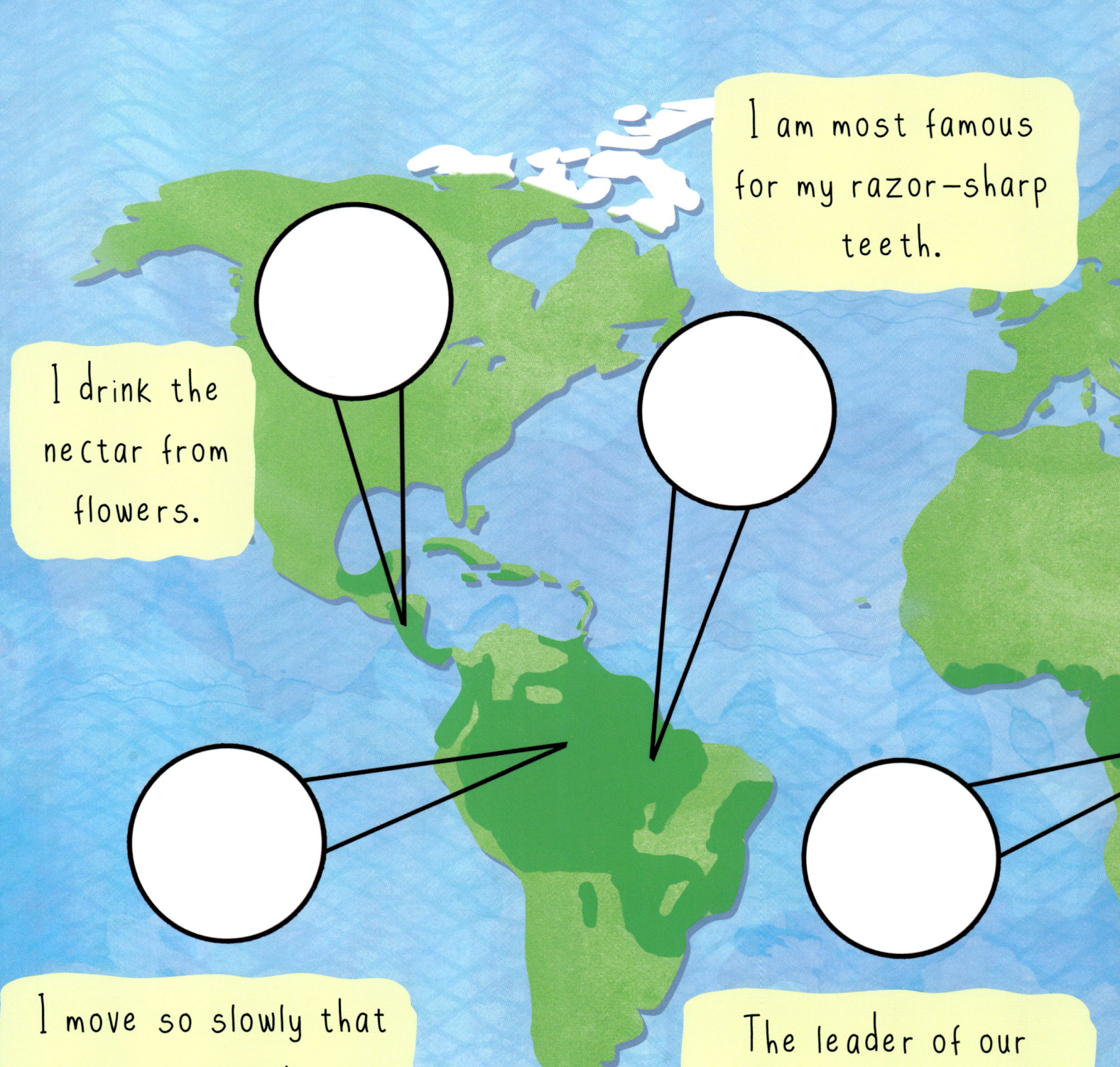

Add stickers from the back of the book to match each creature to its homeland. You can use the clues below to help you.

I stay with my mother until I'm seven years old, and we swing through the trees together.

My roar can be heard over two miles away.

I wave my long furry tail in the air like a flag.

I can't fly, and I lay bright green eggs.

The island of Madagascar is full of amazing plants, animals and birds, and 70% of the species that live here are not found anywhere else on Earth. Wow! Look at this busy Madagascan jungle and see if you can spot the items listed below.

Can you find...

3 ring-tailed lemurs

2 chameleons

A tiny, spiky tenrec

A purple orchid

A red tomato frog?

Marco and Amelia have come to Rwanda in search of mountain gorillas. They have found this group, called a troop, in a clearing high up in the Volcanoes National Park. Use your stickers to add more gorillas to this troop.

The jungle is full of strong, green vines that grow between the trees and wrap around their trunks. But some of these vines are more lively than others! Can you spot which of these vines are snakes in disguise?

Today, Marco and Amelia are up high near the tree tops. This is called the canopy, and it's the busiest part of the rainforest. Up here, you'll find curious monkeys, beautiful birds and butterflies and lots more. Use your stickers to fill the canopy with creatures.

Our two explorers have spotted a toucan high in a tree. Marco thinks it looks so funny with its black feathers and giant, bright beak. Here's how you can draw a toucan.

1 Use a pencil to draw a circle for the head, and a slanted oval for the body.

2 Add a curved triangle for the start of the toucan's beak, and connect the head and body.

3 Add tail feathers and zig zags for the feet. Next add a wing and a line from the top of the head to the outer edge of the body.

4 Add detail to the beak and draw a beady eye. Draw around the outline of your toucan with a pen and erase the pencil lines.

Amelia has started to draw another toucan here. Can you help her to finish it off?

The jungle is home to hundreds of species of butterfly, from those that are clever at camouflage, to those that love to show off with big, bold wings. Can you spot the matching pairs?

Marco and Amelia are taking a trip down the mighty Amazon River. There are all sorts of animals, birds and fish to look out for, including the slithery green anaconda, which is the biggest snake in the world! Use your stickers to complete the scene.

Macaw parrots of the Amazon rainforest love to lick the salty clay from these cliffs. It adds important nutrients to their diet.

Can you spot eight differences between these two parrot pictures?

Marco wants to cross this river with Amelia, a bag of treats for the camp and a monkey he's made friends with. The boat is only big enough to carry Marco and one other thing, so he will need to make several trips. He can't leave Amelia alone with the monkey because she's a bit scared of it. He can't leave the monkey alone with the treats as it will eat them! How can he get everyone across the river?

These tiny hummingbirds flap their wings about 70 times a second as they fly from flower to flower in search of nectar. Use your pens to make these birds extra bright.

TR_PIC_L _CRE_CH
_W_

API

R_D-€y__ T_E_ F__G

At night, the jungle is alive with croaks, hoots, snufflings and scuttlings as the nocturnal creatures wake up. Amelia and Marco are on a night-time hike. Can you fill in the blanks and name the creatures they see?

O__lO_

AR__Dl_lO

TA__N_UlA

Bengal tigers are found in the forests of Asia. They are fierce predators and they're also incredibly rare. Experts think there are only around 2,000 left in the wild. Use your felt-tip pens and the key below to shade in the numbers and make this scene come to life.

KEY

1. Dark green
2. Pink
3. Brown
4. Black
5. Orange
6. Yellow
7. Purple
8. Light green

The jungles of Southeast Asia include some seriously big, bad bugs of all shapes and sizes, from giant blue tarantulas, to blood-sucking leeches, to millipedes with hundreds of legs. Add more creepy-crawly stickers to this page.

Tiny termites are amazing builders. The huge mounds they make from dirt contain complex networks of tunnels and chambers. Can you help the little red termite get from the top to the bottom, where some tasty leaves are waiting?

Start

The pitcher plant attracts bugs with a sweet smell. They slip down the insides of the plant and drown in a pool at the bottom before being turned into bug soup!

This is the beehive ginger plant, which can be used to treat burns.

Some giant orchids can weigh more than one ton and have more than 10,000 flowers!

This rafflesia has a huge bloom, but it's most famous for its smell of rotting meat. Yuck!

The world's rainforests contain some incredible plants. Use your pens to design some fantastic, fragrant or frightening flowers and plants of your own.

Beautiful hibiscus flowers are sometimes called shoe flowers, because they can be used as a type of shoe polish!

The rainforest is full of beautiful and breathtaking things, but it can be a dangerous place too. See if you can match up each of the deadly creatures below with the correct fact about it.

A.

1. I bite my prey and drink its blood.

2. I use my sharp claws to snatch monkeys and parrots right out of the trees.

B.

C.

3. I may be small, but I am poisonous enough to kill ten men!

4. My sting is one of the most painful in the world, and lasts for up to 24 hours.

D.

E.

5. I live in rivers and stun my prey with an electric shock.

6. I hunt alone and like to eat monkeys, deer and fish. My jaws are so powerful that I can crunch bones.

F.

G.

7. I usually eat fish, but if I'm hungry enough I might take a bite out of you!

8. My jaws are stretchy so I can swallow my food whole, no matter how big it is.

H.
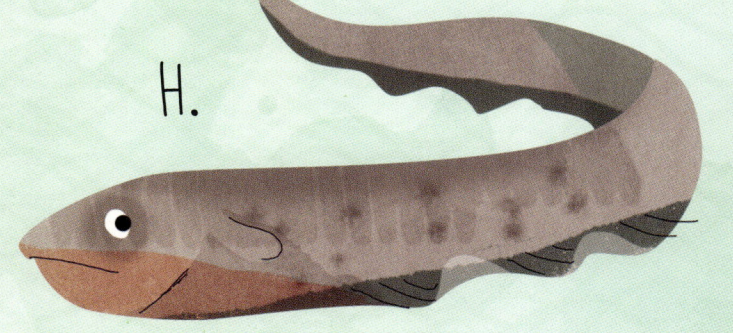

These reddish-brown apes are orangutans, and they live in the forests of Borneo and Sumatra. They swing from tree to tree and build nests to sleep in. Add more amazing apes to this scene with your stickers.

Australia's Daintree rainforest is the oldest in the world. Large birds called cassowaries walk among the trees looking for tropical fruit that has fallen to the ground. Use your stickers to add more cassowaries and tasty fruit for them to find.

The rainforest might seem like a faraway place, but it's really important to your life at home. Take a look at Amelia's shopping bag and you'll see just how many everyday things come from the world's forests. Can you finish them off with your pens?

How about a cup of tea? Tea leaves are grown in tropical regions around the world.

Chocolate comes from the seeds of the cacao tree.

A type of rainforest plant oil is used in toothpaste to make it foam and bubble in your mouth.

Spicy black peppercorns are the berries from a jungle plant.

Rainforest fruits and plants such as brazil nut and passion fruit are used in lots of shampoos!

This rainforest creature is famous for being sloooow. It hangs from tree branches and spends most of its time asleep. Join the dots to find out what it is.

It's time to make camp for the night. It might be hard to get comfortable in a hammock, but it will protect you from some of the creepy crawlies on the rainforest floor! Finish Marco and Amelia's camp with your stickers.

Are you ready for the Jungle Awards? These creatures might not be the biggest or the fastest, but they've got some skills worth shouting about. Let's see who our winners are...

ALMOST INVISIBLE

The glass frog has a see-through belly, making it harder to spot among the leaves.

The basilisk lizard can run on two legs, and the long toes on its feet mean it can run across water without sinking. Wow!

WINNER ON WATER

STRONGEST SPINE

The hero shrew, found in Africa, has a backbone so strong that an adult human could stand on it without hurting it!

The blue bird of paradise pulls out all the moves when he's trying to impress a lady! He hangs upside down and shakes his bright blue feathers.

GREATEST DANCER

FANCIEST FINGERWORK

The shy aye-aye has one very long finger that it uses to reach inside tree trunks and scoop out grubs to eat.

Leaf-cutter ants work together to bring pieces of leaf back to their colony. They use the leaves to grow fungi, which they eat.

BEST TEAMWORK

Can you find these items from your jungle adventure hidden in the grid below?

MACAW

SLOTH

TOUCAN

A	Z	L	E	E	N	A	C	A	M	A	W
D	H	P	I	A	H	N	A	R	I	P	R
N	J	T	F	M	T	X	O	N	A	C	O
O	V	O	T	N	U	Q	M	T	Y	W	U
C	M	T	O	J	L	E	M	U	R	A	E
A	S	A	U	T	H	O	S	L	W	X	F
N	W	T	C	E	M	U	W	A	R	Y	J
A	H	E	A	A	U	O	T	I	C	K	X
C	T	P	N	I	W	S	P	R	U	R	T
E	O	R	A	G	R	C	S	L	O	T	H
L	N	A	T	U	G	N	A	R	O	C	G
P	I	R	A	B	V	W	E	O	P	Y	S

PIRANHA

ORANGUTAN

LEMUR

ANACONDA

Marco and Amelia have had an amazing time on their tropical trip, but now it's time to leave the jungle and explore somewhere new. Will you join them on their next adventure?

Answers

Check all your answers here... but no cheating!

World Map

Madagascar

Sneaky Snakes

There are eight snakes!

Matching Pairs

Spot the Difference

River Crossing

Marco takes the monkey across the river and leaves it on the other side. He comes back and takes the bag of treats across, then brings the monkey back with him. Next he takes Amelia across the river, leaves her on the other side and finally he comes back for the monkey. Now everyone is safely across the river.

Night Hike

* Ocelot
* Red-eyed tree frog
* Tarantula
* Tropical screech owl
* Tapir
* Armadillo

Termite Maze

Deadliest

1. C   5. H
2. D   6. A
3. B   7. E
4. F   8. G

Dot To Dot

Word Search

Stickers to dress up Marco and Amelia

Stickers for high up in the canopy

Stickers for big, bad bugs

Stickers for the orangutans in Borneo